THE ONE THING TO MANIFEST THE LIFE YOU DESIRE

THE ONE THING TO
MANIFEST
THE LIFE YOU DESIRE

Sanjeev jain

Worldwide Published by
Pendown Press

PENDOWN PRESS
An ISO 9001 & ISO 14001 Certified Co.
Regd. Office 2525/193, 1st Floor, Onkar Nagar-A,
Tri Nagar, Delhi-110035
Ph.: 09350849407, 09312235086
E-mail: info@pendownpress.com
Branch Office 1A/2A, 20, Hari Sadan, Ansari Road,
Daryaganj, New Delhi-110002
Ph.: 011-45794768
Website: PendownPress.com

First Edition: 2021

ISBN: 978-93-89601-87-9

Layout and Cover Designed by Pendown Graphics Team
Printed and Bound in India by Thomson ress India Ltd.

CONTENTS

About the Author

Sanjeev is an MBA from the Indian Institute of Foreign Trade, Delhi.

He is married to Ekta and is blessed with two sons—Abhinav and Arjun.

It's difficult to say that he derived his hobbies from profession, or profession from the hobbies. He loves Science & Technology, reading Science Fiction and Tech Gadgets.

He has an illustrious career spanning over 20 years. He earlier headed the family business of Fragrance Products & helped it become the largest in its field with a 20 acre plant near Manesar.

Because of his love for Technology, he started TNS (Technology Never Sleeps) in 2007 which is now a leading provider of Technology Solutions. Sanjeev believes that Technology is no longer a tool, but the transformative power behind Nations & Businesses. **His mission is to help owners of even the most complex businesses, run their business from a smart phone with complete automation!**

He is a distinguished Rotarian having remained President (2014-15) of the prestigious Rotary Club of Delhi Imperial. He is a Level 1 Major Donor & Paul Harris Fellow. He has helped set up social projects, such as Solar Power & Computer Labs for village schools, vocational training schools, etc.

He is the Past President of the BNI's Empezar Chapter, which is one of the best performing BNI Chapters in Delhi NCR with over 80 highly credible members.

He is regarded as one of the best Past Presidents of BNI's Empezar Chapter. During his tenure, it became one of the best performing BNI Chapters in Delhi, NCR with over 80 highly credible members.

His desire is to help Entrepreneurs transform their industry using Technology. He has coached over 3,000 of them including companies like Okaya, Honda, L&T, etc. He has given talks at Rotary, YPO, CII, PHD, NAR, YBLF, AITWA, BGTA, BNI, etc.

WHY PEOPLE DO OR DO NOT ACHIEVE THE THINGS THEY WANT IN THEIR LIFE?

The Principle of 2 powers

Did you ever wonder what actually makes things happen in your life? Can you take a minute to think about the power which has helped you achieve whatever you have created in your life till now ? The very first power is "You". Do you remember the time when you really wanted to get something done on a particular day but couldn't do it? If you are really determined to do something on a particular day, I am sure that most of the times, you will get it done. Whatever you have really committed to, don't you manage to finish it ?

On some days, it may happen that you have to fly out in the evening for an important meeting or holidays, but you still have lots of work at office. Are you able to finish all the work on time and still make it to your flight? Do you know why? The reason is that you have limited time, so you have made a mental note of the things that you need to finish and you have a very clear focus on what all you need to get done. This led me to an important realisation that - "I am an amazing person and whatever I commit to, I will get it done !".

Let us now talk about the other power. Did things happen in your life that you really wanted but did not know how to make them happen ? This power helps you attain things based on your desires.

Let me share my own life's example — how this power helped me set up my Technology business in a way that I could never imagine.

I was a student of science till 12th standard, but shifted to commerce stream because of my father's recommendation to help him with our family business of manufacturing and export of fragrance products such as agarbattis and candles. After completing my B.Com (Hons.) from Shaheed Bhagat Singh College, I did my MBA from the Indian Institute of Foreign Trade, (IIFT), Delhi which specialises in international business. After completing my MBA, I joined my family business in 1996 and nearly doubled its revenues every year.

My father was running a small handicraft business since 1991. Being very much interested in computers, I was looking for the ways to use Technology to help grow this business. During the summer holidays, I had an opportunity to visit my aunt in Canada. During that trip, I found that the products there had very good packaging, while the ones being exported by us were very shabby looking. I purchased many samples of such products with good packaging, and used my technical skills to upgrade the packaging of our products to International standards. Because of this, customers liked the products and we started receiving huge orders worth several crores of rupees.

I automated the production using the latest techniques that I got from China, Japan and Taiwan. Traditionally, product such as agarbatti and candles in India are made by hand, but by using machines, we were able to get extremely good quality in very large quantities, sufficient to supply to worldwide retailers such as Walmart, Target, Carrefour, Tesco, Asda, etc. In fact we even became the OEM (Original Equipment Manufacturer) for the Mangaldeep brand of Agarbatti owned by ITC. To manage the business efficiently, I set up an ERP(Enterprise Resource Planning) program and an intranet way back in the year 2002.

Things were going well with my fragrance products business, but, because of my love for science and technology, I was never really satisfied. The turning point came in my life on a late evening in April of 2006. I had just returned from Hong Kong after attending the International Trade Fair where we had participated and met all our clients. I was sitting in my office with a junior sampling in charge and getting samples ready to send to various customers for approval. With great hesitation he asked my permission to say something. This is what he said- "Sir, I feel that you are a genius with computers; shouldn't you be doing some work related to technology?" I was really shocked to hear this coming from such a junior employee. Even he could see that my passion is technology, while I was continuing to fool myself making candles and agarbatti. This really disturbed me and further deepened my desire to start a business based purely on technology.

It was September of 2006 and I was busy preparing for the upcoming Indian Handicrafts and Gifts Fair. This again is one of the most important events for fragrance products business, with buyers coming from all over the world to attend the same. There was a lot of work, I had to get the latest samples prepared according to the new themes for the season, get ready the design for booth at the trade show, send invitations to all the buyers and buying agents, etc.

Out of the blue, I received a call from one of my father's friends who wanted me to visit to help him with his new business venture. Due to my preoccupation with the upcoming trade show, initially I kept ignoring him. However, after getting some serious reprimand from my father, I was forced to go and meet him at his new office in Okhla Phase 1.

When I visited his office, I was pleasantly surprised to see a beautifully designed office with energetic staff going about their daily work. I met Mr Tanwar in his cabin and he warmly welcomed me. He informed me that he has recently acquired a new company that is specialising in IT Infrastructure. This company deals in equipment from renowned companies such as HP, Dell, Cisco, IBM etc. to set up networks, data centers, video communication systems & high end security. Its customers include prestigious companies such as L&T, Honda, VSNL, Reliance, IIT's, Railways, etc. He then asked me if I would like to be a part of his new venture and to help him run the same efficiently, as I understand technology in a much better way. This was of course a non-question for me. Within 2 months, I had handed over the reins of the existing business to my younger brother who had just completed his MBA from Bradford, UK. Another surprise came after 4 months, when, Mr Tanwar offered to transfer the entire business to me as he became interested in another large venture and did not have sufficient time to devote to both the businesses.

So, just in a matter of a few months I was living the life of my dreams, doing the business, I would love to do. Wouldn't you say that this was simply a divine gift? I had absolutely no idea how to start a new technology business and it simply fell into my lap in a way that I couldn't even imagine. In a way you could say that I manifested the business from my desires.

This now brings us to the second power that can help you realise your goals & dreams in life - "The Power of Manifestation". This power can be simply explained by using a famous dialogue of actor Shahrukh Khan from his movie "Om Shanti Om" -

"Itni Shiddat se maine tumhe paane ki koshish ki hai, ke har zarre ne mujhe tumse Milane ki saazish ki hai. Kehte hain ki...agar kisi cheez ko dil se chaaho to puri kayanat usey tumse milane ki koshish mein lag jaati hai."

In simple English, it means that if you really want something from the bottom of your heart, then the entire universe will try to help you get the same. This power is also known as the "Law of Attraction". Whatever you really want and think about, will be attracted to you & will manifest on its own.

Universe is extremely powerful; it can as easily manifest for you a business worth thousands of crores or something as simple as a cup of coffee . I would highly recommend that you read the book called - "The Secret", by Rhonda Byrne. This book is also available as a movie which you can also find on YouTube in Hindi as well as in English.

To some of you this may seem like hocus-pocus, but now this has been established firmly by the men of science through a principal called - "Reticular Activation."

Our minds are incredibly sophisticated. We can sort through billions of bits of data at any given time. And for some reason, so we don't short circuit, we have to organise that data.

The Reticular Activating System assists with that.

The Reticular Activating System (RAS) is a collection of nerves in your brainstem that filters out unnecessary information so that the essential stuff makes it through.

You get what you focus on!

The RAS is the reason why when you learn a new word, you start hearing it everywhere. It's the reason that you can disregard a crowd full of talking people, however immediately snap to attention when somebody mentions your name or something that at least resembles it.

Your RAS takes what you concentrate on and develops a filter for it. It then sorts through the data and delivers only the parts that are essential to you. All of this happens without you noticing, naturally. The RAS programs itself to work in your favor without you actively doing anything. Pretty awesome, right?

Similarly, the RAS seeks data that validates your beliefs. It screens the world through the parameters you give it, and your beliefs form those parameters. If you think you are weak at giving speeches and presentations, you probably will be. If you feel you work efficiently, you probably do.

Everything in your life is a reflection of your inner state.

The Reticular Activating System helps you see what you would like to see and in doing this, influences your actions.

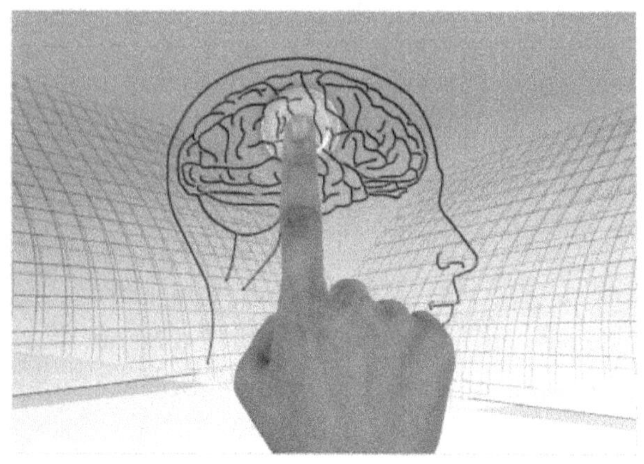

Some people suggest that you can train your RAS by connecting your subconscious thoughts to your conscious thoughts. They also call it "**setting your intent.**" This simply means that if you focus hard on your goals, your RAS will reveal the persons, data and opportunities that help you achieve them.

In conclusion, I would like to say that "First Power" that helps you achieve anything is the power of "**Self**" - your own commitment. "**Second Power**" that actually makes anything happen in your life is the power of "**Manifestation**", whether you attribute the same to God / the Universe / or the Reticular Activation System.

Let us take a stock of what you believe in and check if it can help or hinder you in using these two powers to your advantage.

- What you think about successful people?

  a. They are disgusting

  b. They are lucky

   c.   They are an inspiration

   d.   They are superficial

- You believe in:

   a.   Destiny

   b.   Hard work

   c.   Hard work, Mental preparation and Consistency

   d.   Luck

- You curse your Luck because:

   a.   You are born in a poor family

   b.   You did not get fruits of your hard work

   c.   You never curse your Luck

   d.   Your feel that somehow your stars are not right

- What you think about money?

   a.   It is not something we should hanker after

   b.   It can't buy happiness

   c.   Not everything but important thing to have

   d.   Too much money can corrupt you

- What do you think about success?

   a.   It is something elusive/like a mirage

   b.   Being successful is not the only thing in life

   c.   Success is about getting recognition, love and respect

   d.   To a large extent your stars control your success

- What do you think about time ?

    a.   It is something difficult to manage

    b.   Too many things and not enough time

    c.   It's important to plan ahead as everything takes time

    d.   Following a set schedule makes you feel constricted.

Note: If the answer of most of my questions is (c) that means you are on the right track. If it is not, you will need some training to mold your thoughts to some extent so that this book could prove to be more beneficial for you.

WHY DO THESE POWERS FAIL YOU?

Now, we come to the question as to how well these powers are working in your life? Are you really able to use them to create the life of your dreams? Are they not really working out as expected? Is there something that is stopping them from working? What could it be? Could it be you, who is to blame?

Are you simply being too lazy to use these amazing powers?

Anything worthwhile, doesn't come easily; it and requires a lot of hard work. You know very well that if you commit to doing a certain task on a particular day, you may end up doing it. This means "Hard Work", so what is the best way of avoiding it - "Not deciding what needs to be done!". So, you go through each day cherry picking the easiest tasks and mindless work (like phone calls, meetings, checking bills, etc.) while keeping aside the "Important Work" for "someday" when you are relatively free and can give it the proper attention it deserves. From your experience you know that this "**someday**" is very elusive and may never come.

This is the easiest way for you to - "**Not achieve your goals and dreams that you have been longing for**". Since you have failed to declare/commit to yourself what needs to be done, there is no way for the "**First Power**" - the power of your own commitment to help you achieve your goals.

Everything seemed easy, but you simply failed to take the required action when it was due and that was the reason behind so many failures.

At the same time, this inaction on your part also causes the second power to fail. Since you haven't decided what you really want, the second power - "**Law of Attraction**" has no way to help you. As per the "**Law of Attraction**" - whatever you really want and think about, will be attracted to you & will manifest on its own.

Another important thing to think about is to consider for a moment that God Himself has come to you in your dreams to grant your wishes and is asking you -

My Child! What do you want from today?

What do you want from tomorrow?

What do you want from this week?

What can I do for you this month?

What do you want to achieve this year?

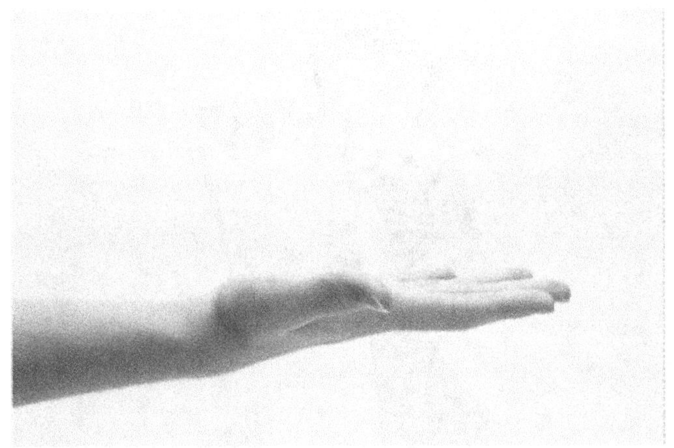

However, you fail to answer these questions because you are not able to decide what you really want from today/ tomorrow/this week/this month and so on and so forth. Since you consistently fail to answer these questions, in effect, you are preventing God or Universe from trying to help you achieve your desires.

It is like going to a restaurant and when the waiter comes to take your order - you are silent. You are happy with a glass of water that is there on the table and come back without eating anything. In fact two waiters — one the "Power of Self", and second, the "Power of Manifestation" were there who kept waiting for your answer.

Do you see the irony? While on your one hand you are extremely frustrated, because you are not getting the things that you want, on the other hand you are simply failing to ask for them or declare whatever you wanted to the only two powers that could have helped you get them.

How to Create your Own Life—Lifestyle Design

Everyday you wake up, go to work and come back after achieving little or no results. Now that I have your attention, would you like to know how to easily declare your wishes day by day, week by week to yourself and without fail? However, before we can do this you need to make a self ready. You need to come out of your comfort zone . Either, you have to give up your dreams, or, commit yourself to do whatever it takes to achieve them. Life does not happen to you, you make it happen!

You create your own life, you have the power to design what your life will look like tomorrow, day after, this week, this month, this year and in the next few years . This is also known as "**Lifestyle Design**" - living the life designed by you! To start on this journey you now need to make a commitment that you will take charge of your own life, live it the way you want, and create the results that you cherish and desire.

All of this can be easily achieved through a simple technology— "The Calendar". Like physical objects such as a bottle of water needs some space to keep them, in the same way any task that you wish to get done needs a specific day and time when it will be worked upon. There is no point in simply noting down your tasks in a "To do list". It is now a well acknowledged fact that "To do lists" do not work. Most of the top entrepreneurs like—Elon Musk, Sir Richard Branson, Jeff Bezos etc. have shunned the to do list in favour of the Calendar. An important task that needs to be done without having a specific time/date attached to it is like having an expensive computer equipment without any power. I would like to quote a famous saying -

"**To do lists are a graveyard of your most important tasks which you never got the time to do.**"

So, if there is anything you really wish to complete, you must declare it on a specific date and time on your calendar. Calendar is not just a simple tool for planning and scheduling, it is much more. It is a tool for **"Commitment"** and **"Manifestation"**. You can also say that it is a **"Life Creation Tool"** - that helps you **design your life** - hour by hour and day by day.

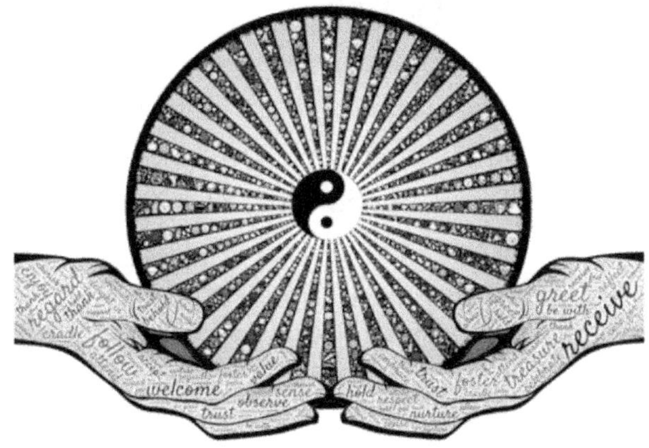

Let us now talk about the five steps that you need to follow to use your "Life Creation Tool" effectively -

The first step you must commit to use this incredible tool without fail. I have made a small commitment to myself and I want you to follow this as well. I have committed to myself that - **"I shall not enter my office on Monday morning till my week is fully planned"**. I follow this rule diligently, in fact, many a times, I find myself sitting outside the office in my car, completing my weekly schedule on my laptop before I can enter my office. With regular practice I have become so good, that usually, my weekly review and planning is already done by Sunday 8:00 a.m.

Trust me this simple commitment can change your life! Once you have made this commitment, I will now highlight some important things to keep in mind to effectively plan your week and pitfalls that you can avoid to ensure that you stick to the plan.

Step1-Use a Capture Tool

The worst thing that has happened to us in the modern times is that too many things are coming at us all the time - Calls, SMS, Whatsapp, Emails, Meetings etc. These keep us distracted from focussing on what's important. Your mind is a valuable resource and I feel that we end up wasting its power by trying to do or remember too many things at once. This is why I highly recommend to use modern Technology to capture all the things that you want to get done and want to remember. In other words a "Capture Tool".

Besides helping you plan your life, using a "**Capture Tool**" has these amazing benefits:

- **No more Distractions:** The Capture Tool allows you to concentrate on work at hand by simply capturing the new task\call\work so that you can get back to the same at a later time. You are no longer worried that you may forget task.

- **Get real work done:** As I mentioned that your brain is a precious resource, you should not use it like a cheap alarm clock. For remembering things, dates, tasks its best to use the "Capture Tool" which removes the nagging fear that you may be forgetting something really important. This allows you to relax and concentrate on getting important work done.

- **Get others to do the work:** One of the biggest issues of today's hi-tech hyper-impulsive age is that we start taking immediate action on any small task even if there is someone else who is supposed to do it. This is simply because you are afraid that you may forget about it later and it may be best to get it out of the way. However, so many such things pile up and consume your entire day before you know it. One of the biggest secrets to being successful is to "Get work done" not "Do everything yourself". By using a "Capture Tool", you will get an opportunity to review it and see if that work can be transferred to someone who is better suited to the job, saving your valuable time.

- **Reduce communication and meetings:** Excessive meetings\communications is a big time waster. A

"Capture Tool" can help you address this challenge by allowing you to capture all the tasks\work\notes related to a department\project\person. So, whenever you see that person you can go over each item in the "Capture Tool" and avoid multiple meetings\calls to go over each item individually. This itself can save you hundreds of valuable work hours during the year.

You can use any note taking App on your phone as "Capture Tool". However, I would highly recommend using Google Keep as an excellent capture tool because of these features:

1. Available on both PC & Mobile (iPhone/android): Syncs instantly between the two.

2. **Captures all types of information:** Written Notes, Tickable List, Voice Notes (with automated text capture), Drawing, Photos.

3. **Share notes for instant collaboration with anyone:** Shared notes show up on other persons Google Keep and both can make changes.

4. **Time & Place Reminders:** You can set a reminder not only

by date/time, but your Google Keep can also remind you if reach a certain place.

5. **Labels & Colours**: You can label/colour different notes based on your choice for a project/department/person they represent.

6. **Free & Simple**: Apart from the great features mentioned above, Google Keep is free and simple to use. Unlike several task management App with advanced features, it is more effective because everyone can use it!

Let me now give you some brief guidelines on how to use the "Capture Tool" effectively so that it can help you reduce distractions, minimize communication and focus on work that really matter.

You should make a Check list type of note for every Department/Person/Project for which you need to communicate or schedule work often. You should share that particular note using the Share function of Google Keep with the Gmail id of person/persons who should be in loop for that particular note. Whenever you have to note down a work or a reminder pertaining to that person/department/project, simply add a line/item in that particular note.

Delegate Automatically
from Google Keep

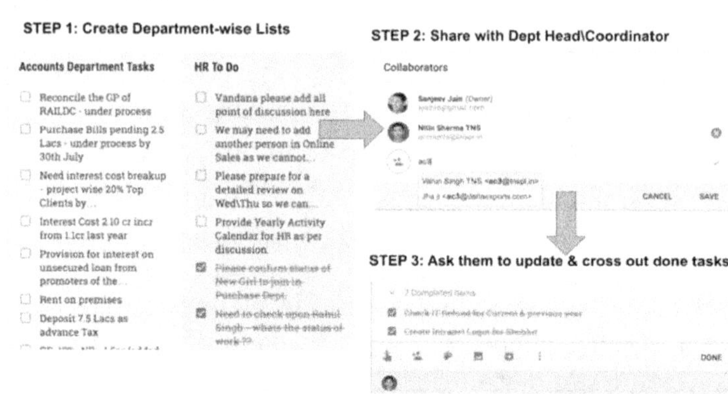

Similarly, you can make a list of tasks or reminders that you need to get done by yourself called "ME". This way you will easily be able to capture any task or reminder for yourself and later schedule the same for an appropriate time.

Now, let's tackle the other issue—getting yourself and others to check the Capture Tool on a consistent basis to ensure that the work gets done and at the same time reducing back-and-forth communication by more than 50 percent. Firstly, get the Google Keep App installed on the phones of your colleagues or employees and give them basic training on how to use the same. Secondly, whenever you meet them in the office, take out your phone and open the note pertaining to that person before you start any discussion. Now, go over each item in the note and update the status. This helps you in many ways -

1. This will ensure that none of the items get missed out from your discussion.

2. You will reduce the need to communicate often and you will be interrupted less frequently when the other person knows that you will be discussing the entire agenda. You can also ask them to put any point of discussion on the same note.

3. This puts your mind at ease because you know that you will not be missing out on any important task.

4. These lists will help you plan your week in advance.

For more detailed instructions on how to use Google Keep as a perfect Capture Tool you can refer to my online guide at this address www.ceoitbox.com/captool

Step 2

Now, in order to create the week that you want, open your Capture Tool (Google Keep), go over the tasks you have noted down for each category and start transferring each item to your calendar with a specific date and time. You need to review the previous week's calendar, check all those tasks that could not be completed and transfer them to this or next week.

Here are some important tips to ensure that you get the best results when scheduling:

1. It is best to schedule a fixed time for things that need to be repeated on Daily\Weekly\Monthly basis.

2. Do not waste too much time on trying to decide as to which task goes where. Once you have the entire week planned, you can go over the whole thing and make adjustments.

3. Apart from managing your time, it's also important to manage your energy. You should schedule more important and difficult tasks during the first half of the day when your energy level is at maximum. Keep less important and routine type work for the later part of the day.

4. One very important thing to remember while planning your schedule is to **include sufficient buffer time** for each day and the week itself. Task buffers will allow you to complete any unplanned tasks or deal with interruptions. Further they give you a sense for freedom by allowing you certain free slots each day where you can schedule for unexpected work.

   There are 3 types of buffers that you must plan:

   a. **Task Buffer:** You must plan a buffer of 15 to 20 minutes between two tasks to help you attend called return calls & messages or any other small things that you need to get done.

   b. **Daily Buffer:** Also you must keep an hour or two in each day that can help you deal with interruptions. Even if there are no interruptions, you can use the buffer time to complete the tasks scheduled for a future time slot.

   c. **Weekly Buffer:** Similarly, I keep a slot of 3-4 hours free in the middle/later part of the week to allow for any unscheduled but important tasks and events. Also, in case your schedule gets disturbed during the previous days, you can use the buffer time to complete the pending tasks of the week.

5.   To multiply your time, please delegate all work that can be done by your colleagues and get them to plan when they will do the same.

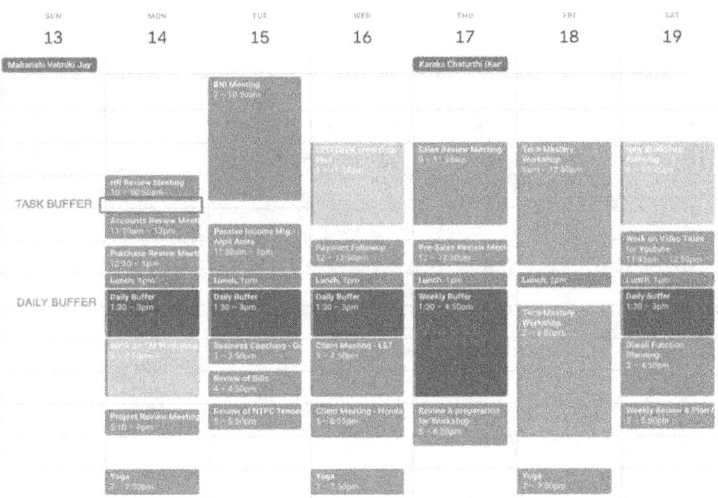

Step 3-Review

It's important for you to see your calendar on a daily basis. I suggest that you sync your phone calendar so that it reminds you of the tasks you have scheduled. It's best to start early and at the end of each day, reflect on what you have accomplished. You should look over the schedule for the next day and then make adjustments based on your achievements for the current day.

To get more tips and techniques on how you can plan your calendar in a better way using Google Calendar please visit my website at www.ceoitbox.com/createlife for step by step instructions and videos.

BONUS: How to use the Calendar to Manifest anything that you want. As I had highlighted earlier, there is a second power that can help you manifest anything that you wish to accomplish- **"The Law of Attraction".** So when you come across a task that you don't know how to accomplish you should still break it down and schedule it for a future but specific date on which you want to complete it. As per the Law of Attraction - the universe will help you find a way for you to complete the task.

For instance, if you wanted to buy a new home, and you are unsure of how to accomplish the same, you can break this task down and schedule it as follows:

1. Will look at various options for my new home - 15th Feb

2. Will finalize my choice - 28th Feb

3. Will set up funding or loan for my home - 15th March

4. Will sign the agreement - 5th April

5. Will move into my new home - 20th April

After you have scheduled these in your calendar, you have completed the first two steps of Manifestation. These are all the steps that you need to follow:

1. Step 1 : Decide what you want.

2. Step 2 : Ask (already done when you schedule it in your calendar)

3. Step 3 : Feel it. Visualize yourself completing the task

on the day when you have scheduled it.

4. Step 4 : Gratitude. Be thankful for all the things that you have accomplished till now.

5. Step 5 : Trust. Trust that the universe will deliver. Don't be sceptical or think of the how, trust in the power of the universe.

EPILOGUE

I hope that you found the content of this short book meaningful and useful in your everyday life. I, as an entrepreneur, did struggle a lot finding my own way around building a successful business. Even after attending huge number of trainings, it was hard to find advice which could be practically applied to solve real business issues. For instance, "The Law of Attraction" - though it's a wonderful concept, I could hardly find a way to use it to manifest my desires on a day-to-day basis till I experimented by using my calendar for the same.

It is my life's mission to help entrepreneurs use cutting edge technology to become Global Business leaders. I believe that technology is the transformative power behind businesses and nations. I have created a complete system to run all the areas of your business with complete automation from just a smartphone. With these innovative techniques, you will be able to automate each and every aspect of running your business. This will allow you to free up your time from routine work and to concentrate on things you enjoy doing and that will actually make your business grow.

I firmly believe - "To achieve success in life one must work hard, however, (with the right tools) struggle is optional."

I invite you to have a look at my website and links given below where you will find invaluable tools and my life's learning on practical steps that can help you immensely in your day-to-day struggle.

www.ceoitbox.com - My website with details of all Business Technology.

www.ceoitbox.com/tool kits - Amazing Toolkits that you can use right now to save huge amount of money, time & headache.

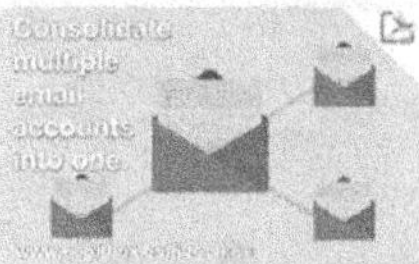

itbx.in/tmbenefits - Learn how to automate each and every aspect of your business.

www.ceoitbox.com/tech-tips - Short tips that make work fun and save you time.

www.ceoitbox.com/Articles - Articles with practical Tools you can use to eliminate struggle from daily business chores.

Here are some images related to these tools:

www.ceoitbox.com/toolkits - Amazing Toolkits that you can use right now to save huge amount of money, time & headache.

itbx.in/tmbenefits - Learn how to automate each and every aspect of your business.

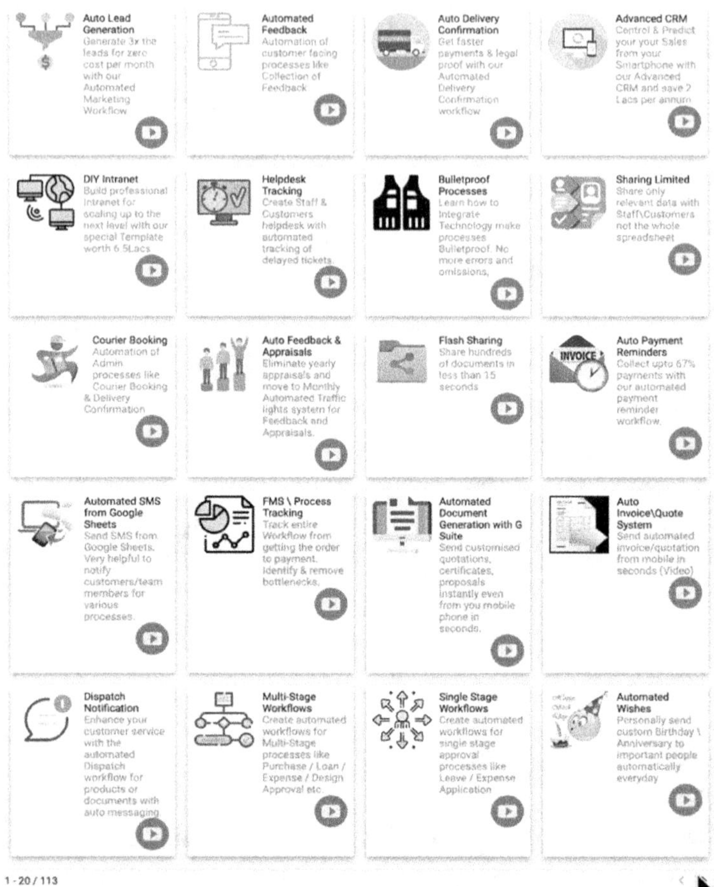

www.ceoitbox.com/tech-tips - Short tips that make work fun and save your time.